Original title:
Paradise on Earth

Copyright © 2025 Creative Arts Management OÜ
All rights reserved.

Author: Evelyn Hartman
ISBN HARDBACK: 978-1-80581-572-3
ISBN PAPERBACK: 978-1-80581-099-5
ISBN EBOOK: 978-1-80581-572-3

Woven Dreams through Garden Gates

Butterflies in top hats dance with bees,
Giggling flowers whisper jokes in the breeze.
The sun wears sunglasses, enjoying the show,
While squirrels plot mischief down below.

Lollipops grow on evergreen trees,
A parade of gnomes sings songs with ease.
Chickens wear sneakers, get ready to race,
In this whimsical world, we find our place.

Return to the Whispering Glades

The trees trade secrets in rustling leaves,
While rabbits play chess, wearing their sleeves.
Mice tell tall tales of pies made of cheese,
And frogs leap for joy, the air filled with wheeze.

Jellybean clouds float in skies so bright,
Where unicorns play tag under starlight.
This place makes you chuckle, puts worries to rest,
A cake made of laughter, the world's very best.

Where Shadows Embrace the Dawn

A raccoon in pajamas dances at dawn,
While owls in bow ties sing a silly song.
The sun yawns wide, stretching its rays,
As shadows giggle in a playful haze.

The grass wears slippers, all comfortable and green,
While ants do ballet, a remarkable scene.
With every soft giggle, the morning's embraced,
In this land of delight, all troubles are chased.

Elysian Dreams

Rainbows sprout legs, and they prance about,
While clouds paint portraits that leave us in doubt.
Dancing donuts jiggle while skydiving pies,
And each little laugh feels like sweet apple pies.

Kites chase each other, spinning in glee,
As bubbles chase dreams, wild and fancy-free.
The moon serves ice cream on a banana peel,
In this place of visions, laughter we steal.

A Haven of Flowing Waters

In a place where ducks wear hats,
And squirrels dance with acrobats.
The rivers giggle and do a twist,
Even the fish can't resist a list.

Trees with arms that give a hug,
Bugs that dance to every tug.
Clouds that sip from straws so tall,
While frogs host parties by the waterfall.

Mosaic of Color in Each Dawn

Every sunrise brings a tease,
Colorful toast sizzling with cheese.
Birds croon tunes, a morning band,
While bunnies frolic, so unplanned.

Flowers gossip in bright hues,
Rabbits in sneakers with rainbow shoes.
The sun yawns wide, its smile bold,
Time for mischief to unfold!

The Lure of Celestial Meadows

In fields where laughter's grown like grass,
Butterflies wear sunglasses with sass.
Kites that giggle as they soar,
Even the daisies start to roar.

Rabbits munching on candy cane,
Chasing dreams down a purple lane.
Bees with buzzes that sound like jokes,
Join the parade of silly folks.

Glimmers of Joy in Every Petal

Petals winking in the breeze,
Tickling noses with sweet tease.
Beetles dressed in polka dots,
Strut their stuff in funny clots.

Sunflowers laugh in radiant sway,
In this goofy garden, come what may.
With every bloom, a chuckle's grown,
Even the earth claims its funny bone!

The Oasis of Wonder

In the garden where bananas grow,
Lizards sunbathe, putting on a show.
Mangoes giggle as they bounce and sway,
Flowers whisper secrets of the day.

The ducks wear hats and strut with pride,
Sipping nectar, they're the fancy kind.
Caterpillars argue who looks the best,
In this wild place, they know no rest.

Dawn's Harmonious Canvas

At dawn, the rooster plays guitar,
Chirping beats that travel far.
Rainbows play hopscotch in the sky,
Even clouds parade, oh my, oh my!

Coffee beans dance in sleepy mugs,
While bees throw rave parties, giving hugs.
The sun wears sunglasses, oh what a sight,
While squirrels throw confetti, pure delight.

Where Love and Nature Dance

Butterflies tango, swirling with grace,
While grasshoppers hop in a lively chase.
The trees tap their roots in a funky beat,
As flowers sway gently, tapping their feet.

Cozy rabbits share carrots, quite bold,
Telling jokes that never grow old.
Bees make playlists of sweet honey tunes,
Under the watch of giggling moons.

The Hidden Haven

In a secret cove, the crabs throw a ball,
With seashells glowing, they invite us all.
Starfish dance like they've lost their shoes,
While dolphins laugh at the ocean's news.

On sunny shores, umbrellas have fun,
Competing with seagulls under the sun.
Kites soar high, tickling the breeze,
In this hidden spot, everyone's at ease.

Eden's Breath in the Whispering Pines

The trees gossip secrets, oh what a show,
With squirrels as actors, putting on a glow.
The raccoons sing ballads beneath the bright moon,
While owls offer wisdom, a quirky cartoon.

A picnic of laughter, with ants in a line,
They march to the rhythm, a dance so divine.
The sun waves goodbye, as fireflies prance,
In this silly haven, we twirl, we dance.

The Palette of Nature's Caress

With flowers like paintings, each color absurd,
They gossip like artists, without a word.
A butterfly fashion show, all flutter and sway,
Nature's wild runway, come see the display!

The bees hum a tune, sweet melodies zoom,
While frogs in the pond plan a salsa costume.
The clouds throw a party, all fluffy and white,
They giggle and tumble, in pure delight.

Tales from the Silk Road of Dreams

On a carpet of wishes, we glide with a grin,
Camel debates fashion, with vibrant chin.
The merchants sell laughter, in jars for a dime,
While foxes in bowties recite silly rhyme.

A caravan of giggles rolls over the sand,
With magic carpets and a wise rubber band.
Stories of shadows dance wildly at night,
In this whimsical marketplace, all feel just right.

Nestled in Nature's Arms

Cuddled by mountains, where the giggles grow,
The brook tells a tale, with a splash and a flow.
The rabbits play hopscotch, in grass that is tall,
While sunbeams play tag, they're having a ball.

With clouds made of candy, we snack on the breeze,
While shadows tell jokes, behind the tall trees.
A haven of chuckles, where laughter is king,
Nature's own circus, let the good times swing!

Garden of Eternal Light

In the garden where gnomes dance,
Sunflowers wear their best pants.
Bunnies hold tea parties with flair,
While squirrels debate who's the heir.

Rainbows slide down buttercup hills,
Bees buzzing like they've got skills.
A frog recites Shakespeare with glee,
Forget the world, come laugh with me!

Echoes of Utopia

In a place where giggles roam free,
Happiness is as bright as a bee.
Clouds are marshmallows, rainbows are fries,
Everyone sports a pair of wise eyes.

Chickens boast with hats on their heads,
While ducks tell tales from their cozy beds.
They play charades with a twist of fun,
Every day brightens with the sun.

The Lush Mirage

Cacti in tutus twirl with grace,
While hippos try to win a race.
Cockatoos sell ice cream, oh what a treat,
In this mirage, everyone's upbeat.

Parrots squawk jokes that make you snort,
And elephants play a raucous sport.
They've got moves that dazzle and shine,
Life's a stage, and all is divine!

Serenity's Embrace

On clouds of candy floss we glide,
Pigs on unicycles joyfully ride.
Butterflies wear glasses, oh so cool,
In this embrace, we're nobody's fool.

Jellybeans rain from the sky so bright,
Chasing dreams in balloons of light.
A turtle plays chess with a cat,
In this scene, there's room for all that!

Tides of Joy and Laughter

In a land where ice cream never melts,
The cows wear shades, it's how they felt.
Drifting on clouds like fluffy ships,
We dive for joy, no need for grips.

Seagulls crack jokes, they steal your fries,
And sandcastles grow with each surprise.
A sun that giggles, a moon that winks,
We dance with flowers, what more to think?

The tide brings in laughter, like waves in glee,
And ticklish shells all gather near the sea.
Where fish wear hats and crabs play guitar,
Every moment here feels like a bizarre.

Pack your bags, forget the fate,
To this funky space, you simply skate.
Where socks and sandals make a trendy pair,
Laughter's a treasure, floating in the air.

Hallowed Grounds of Solace

In a field where broccoli joins the choir,
Lettuce talks gossip by a fire.
Tomatoes wear sunglasses, oh so bright,
While carrots dance under starlit night.

A bench where squirrels tell their tales,
And chipmunks trade their tiny pails.
The breeze brings laughter, like a snooze,
Each sip of lemonade, a joyful muse.

Where daisies debate who's the fairest flower,
And bees wear shoes to flaunt their power.
Tickling the petals, we laugh so loud,
Nature's a jester, drawing a crowd.

So join the revelry, bring your cheer,
To this green stage, where fun is near.
A garden of giggles, wild and free,
With hallowed grounds of sweetness, come see!

Echoes of Laughter in the Breeze

Through the trees, laughter does twirl,
As squirrels wear hats, ready to whirl.
The wind carries giggles, oh what a thrill,
Even the flowers seem to smile at will.

Bubbles float by while frogs try to sing,
As daisies giggle, sharing their bling.
A dance-off with chipmunks, full of glee,
In this wacky world, we jump like a bee.

The sun cracks jokes, and shadows play tag,
Every corner holds a funny brag.
With each rustle, there's a snicker and tease,
Laughter's the language, that's sure to please.

So come join the circus, don't be shy,
With echoes of laughter, we'll soar high.
In this realm where whimsy finds its way,
Get ready for giggles, let's laugh and play!

The Radiance of Gilded Daisies

With daisies dressed in gold, looking fine,
They wink at the sun, and sip on wine.
Butterflies wiggle in a shiny parade,
While ants plan a banquet in the shade.

The grass hums a tune, a ticklish song,
Where everyone knows, we all belong.
Clouds wear silly hats as they pass by,
And trees chuckle softly, oh me, oh my!

An unexpected dance, oh what a sight,
Gilded daisies twirl, morning till night.
With bees playing drums, a band of cheer,
Champagne wishes flow, let's raise a beer!

In this dance and laughter, we gladly bask,
No one needs to ask, just wear a mask!
Join this gathering, full of delight,
Where joy is golden and spirits take flight!

Sunlit Reverie

In a garden where the flowers laugh,
Bees do a jig on a sunlit path.
A cat in shades struts with flair,
While squirrels debate who has the best hair.

Tomatoes wear hats, red and round,
They gossip about the ants they found.
With each giggle, the sun spills gold,
In this silly realm, lives never get old.

Spirit of the Sacred Grove

In the grove where the trees wear shoes,
And daisies gossip, sharing their views.
A frog in a tie tells dad jokes,
While fireflies dance in little spokes.

The owls chuckle, wise and spry,
As rabbits debate on how to fly.
Beneath the canopy, laughter flows,
Where even the grumpy hedgehog knows.

Infinite Horizons

On a beach where the waves do cartwheels,
Seashells play poker, sharing their deals.
Witty crabs create fashion shows,
With outfits made from those beachy clothes.

Kites soar high with a cheer and a twist,
While a sandwich claims, 'You can't resist!'
With laughter bubbling from way up above,
This jolly scene fits like a glove.

The Enchanted Refuge

In a nook where the clouds sip tea,
A mouse in a coat plots to be free.
The flowers speak in rhymes and puns,
While turtles race for fun in the sun.

Pixies play pranks, sprinkling dust,
While the wise old owl gives tips to trust.
In this cozy haven, all is bright,
As laughter rings out into the night.

The Elixir of Life

In a garden where laughter grows,
The sun wears shades and strikes a pose.
Flowers sip from coffee cups,
While bees play hopscotch and do push-ups.

The fountain giggles, splashes cheer,
It whispers jokes for all to hear.
Squirrels hold court in the shady trees,
As butterflies dance in the soft breeze.

Odd clouds play tag, so fluffy and white,
While mountains wear tinfoil hats, oh what a sight!
A rainbow rides a bike through the sky,
Singing silly songs as it whizzes by.

And here our hearts do twirl and spin,
Sipping joy from life's great tin,
In this place where cheer is rife,
We find the true elixir of life.

Architectural Dreams in Bloom

In a town with houses made of cheese,
Where mice take classes and bake with ease.
Roofs painted with jellybeans and sprinkles,
As giggles echo and sunshine twinkles.

The streets are paved with gingerbread,
Where gumdrop gardens get plenty of bread.
Fanciful fountains squirt soda pop,
While ice cream cones atop rooftops plop.

In this place where dreams have fun,
Balloons hold meetings under the sun.
Chairs made of cupcakes and tables of pie,
Laughing together as kites fly high.

Architects sketch with crayon delight,
Building castles that twinkle at night.
Every corner a whimsical sight,
In this land, everything feels just right.

The Blissful Cove

At the cove where seagulls sing,
Laughter drips from every swing.
The sandcastle towers wear leafy crowns,
While starfish gossip in colorful gowns.

Palm trees play cards with the ocean waves,
While crabs in sunglasses misbehave.
The sun steals cookies from the tide,
As dolphins cheer in a splashing ride.

Beach balls bounce like happy pups,
As clams compete in hula hoops.
Sunsets bring a silly parade,
With parrots in tuxedos swinging a spade.

In this cove, joy leaps and dives,
Where the unexpected truly thrives.
Each moment a gift, a chuckle or two,
Here's to the fun and the sunny view!

Timeless Echoes in the Valley

In a valley where giggles dance in the air,
Where time takes a break and just doesn't care.
Trees hum melodies, roots tap their feet,
As shadows play tag on the warm earth's sheet.

Mountains dressed up in powdered sugar,
Invite the sun to come and figure.
Clouds tell tales of cheese and pie,
While flowers laugh as butterflies fly.

Echoes of fun bounce from hill to hill,
Where laughter and joy are never still.
Crickets join in a ribbiting cheer,
As friends gather 'round, for wine, or a beer.

Here worries dissolve like candy in tea,
In this timeless space, we all feel free.
With every heartbeat, joy slaps the ground,
In this valley of echoes, happiness found!

The Eden Beyond Time

In a garden where laughter blooms,
The gnome juggles with furry brooms.
Sunflowers dance, a comical sight,
While squirrels debate who's fastest in flight.

Beneath a tree with candy canes,
A parrot sings plots of poppy lanes.
The bees wear hats, oh what a show,
As the mushrooms conspire to steal the glow.

Rabbits wear slippers, oh what a treat,
As they bicker on who's got the fastest feet.
With every breeze, a chuckle flows,
While the gluten-free bread in the toaster doze.

Time giggles as it swirls around,
With donuts hanging from twinkling ground.
This Eden, a riot of joy and fun,
Where every day feels like a pun-filled run.

Harvest of Peace and Plenty

In fields where joy spills like sweet cider,
The pumpkins grumble, 'We're getting wider!'
Tomatoes blush like teenagers sneaked,
While corn on the cob hurls puns, quite sleek.

Chickens in goggles take the stage,
Debating their future on social wage.
The carrots wear hats, fashionably bold,
While radishes claim they're just too old.

Scarecrows gossip in fashion faux pas,
As the beans protest with a cheery applause.
The sun winks down, a master of cheer,
As fruits compete for the title, 'Most dear.'

At dusk, the harvest dances in rows,
With laughter and pie baking under the bows.
Oh, what a bounty in this funny spree,
Where every crop brings a smile to me!

The Allure of Soothing Whisper

In the breeze, a whisper tickles my ear,
The clouds chuckle, 'Don't take life too dear.'
Butterflies gossip about flirty bees,
As they flutter by with grace and ease.

The brook sings songs of slippery rocks,
While fish tease frogs in eccentric socks.
A breeze croons lullabies to the leaves,
And the oak tree revels in its funny sleeves.

Here, in the laughter of nature's flight,
Morning glories giggle at the first light.
Every rustle and giggle enchants my heart,
In this realm, where sanity's a work of art.

Clouds shaped like marshmallows roam the sky,
Inviting picnics without a shy.
With every glance, a new joke appears,
As the whispering wind spins giggle-filled cheers.

Charmed by Nature's Hand

Hopscotch on moss, what a thrill,
Dancing through shadows, all the time we kill.
The trees wear glasses, quite learned and wise,
While raccoons tease the sun with playful lies.

Flowers wear sneakers, running fast,
They giggle together, outpacing the past.
Ants march like armies, with tiny commands,
While daisies plan parties—imagine their bands!

Clouds do the moonwalk, just for a laugh,
While turtles debate the quickest path.
Each blade of grass sprouts crafty ideas,
In this world where humor rings through the years.

Charmed by the antics of nature's show,
Every corner reveals where laughter will flow.
With every step, a joke's waiting there,
In this delightful world, with wonder to share.

Celestial Shores and Sunlit Paths

On shores where laughter's never shy,
Seagulls wear sunglasses, oh my,
Sandy castles with moat-like depths,
Crabs in tuxedos take their steps.

The sunbeams dance, a merry jig,
Flip-flops squeak, and beach balls dig,
Jellyfish float like balloons, no fuss,
While sunscreen battles cause us to cuss.

Kites on strings like crazy birds,
Tickling noses, won't say a word,
Shells that giggle when placed just right,
Making us laugh from morning till night.

Mermaids giggle, they know the score,
Sandcastles guarded by sand, not war,
Waves that whisper jokes to the shore,
A giggling tide, oh, we want more!

Embrace of the Emerald Valley

In valleys green where cows wear shades,
Grasshoppers dance in funky parades,
Sunflowers laugh, their heads held high,
While carrots chatter about the fry.

Rivers that tickle the rocks with cheer,
Butterflies waltzing, drawing near,
Squirrels gossip about picnic spots,
Under the trees, no one forgets their thoughts.

A breeze whispers secrets, not too loud,
While daisies chuckle in a bright crowd,
Bubbly brooks with laughter collide,
And crickets compose a symphony wide.

Oh, what a place where nature's a jest,
Every critter knows how to rest,
With all this joy, we find our space,
In this green haven, we embrace!

The Symphony of Nature's Heart

Bees on violins buzz a sweet tune,
While frogs in tuxedos croak at the moon,
The wind plays flutes, a breezy delight,
Creating a symphony, oh what a sight!

Drumming logs in the rhythm of trees,
Nature's orchestra, playing with ease,
Foxes with maracas, all in a line,
Strutting their stuff, oh they look so fine!

Clouds float by, a fluffy choir,
With each note, our spirits grow higher,
Sunshine beams like a spotlight's beam,
A hilarious, whimsical dream!

A laughter-filled concert under the sky,
Join us in the fun, oh my oh my,
With nature's heart keeping the time,
Together we dance, in rhythm and rhyme!

Arcadia in a Whisper

Under the moon, the night plays tricks,
Owls wear spectacles, reading the flicks,
Stars giggle softly, twinkling up high,
While crickets chirp gossip, never shy.

Gardens hum with a silvery glow,
Mice in top hats put on a show,
Rabbits debate in scholarly tones,
About the best carrots in their zones.

Fireflies twinkle, they glitter and gleam,
As laughter flows like a bubbling stream,
Whispers of joy float on the breeze,
In this place, tensions all ease.

Every shadow holds a chuckle's embrace,
Nature's secrets, a comical space,
In hushed tones our laughter takes flight,
In this quiet realm, everything's right!

The Dance of Fluttering Leaves

In the garden, leaves do sway,
Dancing wildly in a play.
A squirrel joins with quite a leap,
While kids all giggle, jump, and peep.

The breeze whispers secret tunes,
As butterflies wear silly prunes.
A rabbit moonwalks, what a sight!
While daisies cheer with pure delight.

But wait, a worm joins in the fun,
Wiggling hard, he's second to none.
Together they create a mess,
In this way, they dance and impress!

So come along and twirl around,
Where laughter grows and joy is found.
The world is silly, bright, and free,
In this space of jubilee!

Lush Retreats of Stillness

On a hammock, snores collide,
As birds take bets on who will slide.
A snail speeds by with frantic grace,
While frogs put on their slapstick face.

Trees gossip softly, sharing cheer,
While critters wear their fancy gear.
A lazy cat takes on the throne,
As ants compete for "best choreone."

The sun is shining, life's a joke,
As flowers giggle when they poke.
A hedgehog dons a crown of thorns,
Claiming royalty since the morn!

Each moment's like a circus scene,
Where rustles make the quiet keen.
So grab your shades and soak it in,
In lush retreats, let fun begin!

The Canvas of Wandering Souls

A doodle here, a splash of hue,
With butterflies that laugh at you.
A gnome is painting with a grin,
As grasshoppers do jazz within.

The canvas stretches far and wide,
Where laughter's splattered, colors glide.
A bear wears glasses, quite bemused,
While foxes pose, all art infused.

They trot and twirl, the field's alive,
With crickets leading the jive.
A masterpiece that tickles fate,
Where nonsense reigns, oh isn't that great?

So grab your brush, join the spree,
With giggles that are wild and free.
In this art, no rules to cheer,
Just wandering souls that shed a tear.

Meadows Awash with Daydreams

In meadows wide, the sheep do prance,
While daisies plot their joker dance.
A unicorn trips over its shoe,
As sunflowers giggle, 'Oh, who knew?'

A group of frogs croon silly songs,
While butterflies float all day long.
A turtle forgets what he's said,
As bees just buzz about their bread.

Clouds take bets on who will race,
With squirrels playing chase in space.
A hiccup from a shy red ant,
Turns into laughter, oh what a chant!

So skip along and weave your dreams,
In sly meadows where laughter beams.
In this absurd, whimsical scene,
Let's embrace the wild and serene!

Secrets of the Golden Horizon

In the land where the chickens wear shoes,
The skies are painted with bright polka-dots,
Lemonade rivers flow with the latest news,
And ice cream grows on all the green plots.

Bubbly clouds giggle and float on by,
As coffee beans dance with a jolly twist,
The sun throws a party, oh my, oh my,
While fish with mustaches join in the list.

Pigs ride bicycles, honking with delight,
Bunnies crack jokes, 'What a sight to behold!'
At dusk, the stars twirl in sparkles of light,
While ferrets in tuxedos play poker, so bold.

Every corner's filled with a chuckle so bright,
Tickling the fancies of every guest here,
In this wild realm, there's no need for fright,
Just laughter, sweet laughter, ringing so clear!

Chronicles of the Serene Coast

Seashells gossip, sharing tales in the sand,
With crabs holding court, what a sight to see!
Palm trees are dancing, held by a band,
While seagulls debate who's the best in the spree.

Sunbathers wear shades shaped like a fish,
Sipping coconut smoothies with little umbrellas,
Each wave's a giggle, a salty little swish,
As dolphins play hopscotch with silly fella's.

The beach ball's a star, it rolls with flair,
Bouncing around like a child full of glee,
While sandcastles shout, "Hey, we're all fair!"
And mermaids just laugh, sipping tea by the sea.

With laughter erupting like bubbles up high,
And towels that twirl in a whirl of delight,
This coast is a treasure that money can't buy,
Where mirth meets the waves and all feels just right!

The Oasis of Sighs

In a glen where the cactus wears fancy hats,
And sand dunes beckon with a swish and a sway,
Mice sip on nectar while dodging the bats,
Saying, "What a fine, sunny, whimsical day!"

The palm trees gossip, their leaves in a rustle,
As lizards perform in a show just a treat,
With laughter that bounces, no hint of a bustle,
While jerky old tortoises quickly take a seat.

Cacti surprise with their flowers aglow,
With colors outrageous, a riotous sight,
They gossip in whispers, don't tell what they know,
In this desert realm, it's all pure delight.

Every sigh of relief brings a chuckle anew,
As watermelons dance in a rhythm so groovy,
Here in this spot, there's nothing to rue,
Just giggles and joy, life's funny, and groovy!

Dappled Light through Canopy Dreams

Beneath the great trees, where sunlight beams,
Squirrels wear capes, oh what a grand show!
The leaves are all winking, as if they have schemes,
With acorns proposing a party for all below.

The butterflies flutter, debating their clothes,
"Should we go vintage or sport something new?"
While frogs in their tuxedos strike poses like pros,
Reciting their poems to the critters in view.

Sunbeams are giggling, they tickle the ferns,
And shadows are dancing with wiggles and spins,
The flowers are plotting and waiting their turns,
To outshine the sunlight and claim all the wins.

In this whimsical woodland, laughter takes flight,
With mischief and cheer in every nook and cranny,
Where each moment's wrapped in joy and delight,
And life is a chuckle, all sweet as a canny!

The Allure of Sun-kissed Hills

Oh, the sun-kissed hills are calling,
With waves of grass that keep on sprawling.
Here the cows chew, lost in thought,
While bees dance round, their hive is sought.

Silly goats prance, no sense of time,
While birds compose their merry rhyme.
The sky wears blue, a jester's hat,
A place where joy is just a chat.

The daisies wink in bright delight,
As ants declare a tiny fight.
On every slope, a giggle grows,
With nature's jokes, who really knows?

So roll on down, don't mind the dirt,
In these sun-kissed hills, no pain, just spurt.
With laughter loud, and spirits high,
This is the life, so let out a sigh!

Reverie Upon the Blossom Path

Down the blossom path, we stroll so slow,
Where every flower wears a bow.
The tulips gossip, the daisies tease,
Their colors bright, sure to please.

The bees are busy, with cakes to bake,
While butterflies dance, a funny quake.
A squirrel with acorns plays hide and seek,
Each petal's secret is just for the meek.

Oh, how the fragrance makes us grin,
As we ponder where to begin.
With every step, laughter's near,
On this path, we lose all fear.

So let's not rush, we'll dawdle here,
With every bloom, let's cheer and cheer.
In our mind's feast, let silly reign,
On the blossom path, we'll dance in rain!

The Allurement of Gentle Rain

Gentle rain taps on my window pane,
Like a cheeky kid, it calls my name.
It makes the frogs jump, they can't contain,
In puddles deep, they're going insane.

With umbrellas flipped by a playful gust,
And giggling kids who embrace the dust.
So here we splash, no need to dry,
In every drop, we laugh and sigh.

The flowers grin, their thirst they slake,
While muddy shoes lead me to shake.
Oh, how that raindrop wants to play,
On our heads, oh what a ballet!

So let it pour, we'll dance and twirl,
In our little world, let laughter unfurl.
For in every storm, there's a rainbow's gain,
And joy can sprout beneath the gentle rain.

Serene Horizons of Mind's Eye

In the mind's eye, horizons widen,
With fluffy clouds that seem to bide in.
A laughing moon, it winks at me,
While snickering stars begin to flee.

"Hey there!" says the sun, so bright and bold,
"In this crown of dreams, be not too old."
As shadows prance like kids at play,
Creating forms that lead astray.

The breezes chuckle, whirling around,
As lost ideas scatter the ground.
A fish might fly and a bird might swim,
In this crazy world, my dreams brim.

So bring your quirks to this joyful sight,
Let's frolic wildly, hearts so light.
For in this space of quirky blend,
Every moment feels like a friend.

A Symphony of Blossoms

In gardens where the daisies dance,
The daisies plot their own romance.
They flirt with bees as they sip tea,
In hats and shoes, oh, what a spree!

Tulips gossip with a flair,
They tweet and chirp like they don't care.
With colors bright, a joyful show,
They're strutting like they're in a row.

Roses blush, their thorns on guard,
They jest and jive, they work so hard.
With petals soft, they laugh and spin,
Saying, "Watch us bloom, let the fun begin!"

In this bright patch, life's quite absurd,
Where flowers talk, it's not unheard.
Bring on the laughter, the sunny mirth,
In this wild world, we'll toast to Earth!

The Secret Isle of Tranquility

On an island where the coconuts laugh,
The crabs and seagulls share a gaff.
They sip from shells, play tag in the sand,
With a treasure map drawn by a pirate hand.

Mermaids dance with fish so sleek,
They giggle and wiggle, every week.
With glittered tails and a splashy cheer,
They throw a party when humans near!

Palm trees sway to a calypso beat,
As sun-kissed breezes start to greet.
Banana slugs in tiny shades,
Have laid out snacks that never fade.

In this realm of leisure and jest,
Every creature thinks they're the best.
Join the fun on this sandy spree,
Where 'quit the nonsense' is a decree!

Celestial Shores

On shores where the jellyfish glow,
They move in rhythms like a show.
With umbrellas made of sand and light,
They hold a dance-off, what a sight!

Seagulls strut with swagger and flair,
Chasing their shadows without a care.
With sunglasses on, they call it chic,
Stealing crumbs, they squeak and speak.

The tides chuckle with secrets to share,
As surfers wobble without a care.
In salty splashes, giggles arise,
Making waves under sunny skies.

With every splash and every dash,
They live to play, they live to crash.
With ocean's laughter, the day's complete,
In a world where joy is the ultimate treat!

Whispers in the Meadow

In meadows where the rabbits thrive,
They plan a party, oh how they strive!
With carrot hats and a veggie feast,
They celebrate like a joyful beast.

Butterflies wear polka-dot gowns,
While bumblebees don tiny crowns.
They buzz and flutter, choreograph a dance,
Enticing all to take a chance.

The daisies nod and the grass does sway,
As critters join in on the play.
With tiny drums made of acorn caps,
They host a concert for all the chaps.

Nature chuckles with a gentle breeze,
Tickling petals, with playful tease.
In this grand field, life's like a dream,
With each small creature, creating a scene!

The Blooming Canopy of Timelessness

Under the trees, laughter does stray,
Squirrels have parties, hip hip hooray!
Flowers in tutus, dancing around,
Tickling the bees, such joy can be found.

Pine cones are hats on the heads of the brave,
As crickets recite their songs from a cave.
With mushrooms as tables, they feast on delight,
The squirrels raise a toast to the magical night.

Rainbows like slides stretch down from the skies,
While daisies make crowns, oh what a surprise!
Each wanderer chuckles, tripping on roots,
As fairies in slippers perform their sweet hoots.

So come and enjoy this whimsical cheer,
Where giggles of nature are perfectly clear.
With a wink and a nudge, every moment we savor,
In this everlasting, giggly behavior!

Rivers of Bliss and Starlit Nights

There's a stream of giggles, a river of fun,
Splashing with ducks, a dance on the run.
Stars are the disco balls twinkling above,
While frogs critiqued ballet with a touch of tough love.

The fish wear sunglasses, they swim with such flair,
And turtles slide past in a chill, gentle air.
Every ripple holds secrets, a tickle or two,
As fireflies flash, 'signing' under the blue.

Clouds drift like pillows, soft everywhere,
While laughter of children fills up the sweet air.
The moon's got a grin, as it beams down delight,
Mocking the owls who dream of the night.

A chorus of crickets hum lullabies loud,
To serenade all in a shimmering crowd.
With marshmallow dreams and starry-eyed wishes,
This night is a feast of whimsical dishes!

Song of the Whispering Winds

Winds weave melodies, a comical tune,
Tickling tall grasses, beneath playful moon.
Whispers of secrets swirl 'round the trees,
As branches high-five, swaying with ease.

Clouds play a game of hopscotch and spin,
While thistles wear hats made of spinny old tin.
The shadows are giggling, they dance in delight,
As fireflies play tag in the warm summer night.

Hummingbirds zipping, like planes in a race,
Dandelion fluff drifts, a soft, dreamy space.
Breezes carry chuckles from the flowers below,
As daisies burst into laughter, stealing the show.

With each gust of whimsy, the world shows its face,
A medley of chuckles, the greatest embrace.
Where even the winds join the fun all around,
In the song of existence, pure joy can be found!

The Infinite Enchantment

A land where the laughter is plentiful and bright,
With kittens on scooters zooming left and right.
Rainbows throw parties from morning till dusk,
In this whimsical kingdom, there's never a husk.

Mountains wear hats made of cotton and cream,
While rivers giggle, as they bubble and stream.
The sun plays hopscotch with clouds in the sky,
As butterflies paint murals, oh me, oh my!

Starlight's a sprinkle, a sprinkle of bliss,
Where dreams whisper secrets, not one we'll miss.
Frogs croon ballads with style and a flare,
As ladybugs waltz in intricate pairs.

A bounce in the blossoms, a sway in the breeze,
Every heart finds rhythm, most certainly at ease.
In this place of delight, a chuckle we share,
For magic's a secret we all can declare!

The Embrace of Garden Pathways

Wandering through leafy lanes,
I trip on roots with playful gains.
Flowers giggle as I fall,
A jester's path, the best of all.

Bees buzzing in a cheeky hum,
They steal my snacks, oh, what a fun!
Sunshine plays peekaboo with me,
A silly stroll, pure jubilee.

A squirrel laughs, its acorn prize,
While I get lost in butterfly skies.
Pathways twist like noodle dreams,
Dancing with joy, or so it seems.

Laughter blooms where I do tread,
Garden paths where worries shed.
In every step, a joke unfolds,
Nature's humor never gets old.

Treetops Bathed in Golden Light

High above, where branches sway,
I wave at birds who start to play.
Sunbeams tickle leaves just right,
As I jump up, oh what a sight!

A friendly chipmunk winks at me,
As if to say, "Come join the spree!"
Swinging from a branch so free,
I almost lost my cup of tea.

The sun's a giant, grinning wide,
As I take flight on the slide.
I tumble down a grassy bank,
With laughter ringing, I just sank!

In tree-top homes, so snug and bright,
Nature's punchlines bring delight.
A world so funny, lush, and bold,
In golden light, adventures unfold.

The Splendor of Vibrant Horizons

Colors dance across the skies,
With every hue, the laughter flies.
Funky clouds in stripes and dots,
Nature's palette hits the spots.

Rainbows giggle as they bend,
Their vibrant arcs, a playful friend.
I chase the sun, it plays a game,
Tag, you're it! Oh, what a claim!

Stars poke fun at evening's sprawl,
While I try to catch them all.
They twinkle like a cheeky smile,
Inviting me to dream awhile.

Horizons stretch, a canvas wide,
With every sunset, joy and pride.
In colorful splendor, life's a cheer,
Make a wish, the sky will hear!

Harmony Among the Flowers

In fields where blooms have come to play,
Petals tease the breeze all day.
Daisies whisper, "Look at me!"
While sunflowers strut, full of glee.

Butterflies make fancy flits,
As I join in with silly skits.
Tulips chuckle in the sun,
Their colors bright, oh what fun!

A bumblebee, my buzzing pal,
Buzzes jokes; I'm his biggest gal.
We share the nectar, sweet delight,
In this garden, all feels right.

Here, laughter sprouts from every stem,
Nature's humor, a cherished gem.
Among the flowers, joy abounds,
In harmony, silliness surrounds.

Twilight's Gentle Glow

Sunsets tease the sleepy bees,
Chasing dreams on fluffy trees.
Wink at stars, they wink right back,
Dance in slippers, never lack.

Fireflies join the silly waltz,
Spin your partner, no big faults.
Giggling grasshoppers play along,
To the rhythm of a silly song.

Silly shadows start to prance,
Underneath the moon's wide glance.
Laughter echoes through the night,
In this glow, everything feels right.

A Realm Beyond the Clouds

Up high where the cloud-fluffs float,
Socks on heads, we sail and gloat.
Catch a rainbow, make it dance,
Or share a lollipop romance.

Giant marshmallows hold our weight,
As we giggle and contemplate.
A lemonade waterfall, so sweet,
Sip it slow, it can't be beat.

Silly birds wear hats and ties,
Sprinkling jokes from sunny skies.
When clouds grow tired, we take a nap,
Resting on our cotton trap.

The Color of Happiness

Dancing in a field of hues,
Where smiles sprout like vibrant views.
Painted flowers tickle toes,
While giggling rhymes blow in the prose.

A bubble bursts with squeals of glee,
Splashes of laughter like the sea.
Wiggly worms in polka dots,
Invite us to their tiny spots.

Puppies consider comedy,
As cats roll their eyes, oh can't you see?
In this palette, life's a jest,
Tickling hearts, we're truly blessed.

Crystal Waters and Golden Sands

On shores where turtles wear sun hats,
And crabs dance as aquatic spats.
Sandy castles rise and fall,
As seagulls shout a beach ball call.

Mermaids giggle in the tide,
While fishes watch from the side.
Goldfish offering goofy waves,
As we chase the sun's hot braves.

Laughter bubbles in the breeze,
Sand between our toes with ease.
In tides of joy, we take a stand,
In this place so joyful and grand.

Echoes of Serenity in Every Breeze

In the garden where the daisies sing,
A cat wears shades, thinks it's a king.
Butterflies dance with socks on their feet,
While ants throw a rave, what a funny tweet!

Laughter bubbles from the bubbling brook,
Fish wear bow ties, just take a look.
Even the frogs have a jumpy feat,
Hopping in rhythm to a disco beat.

The sun shines bright on this silly spree,
As squirrels juggle acorns with glee.
Tulips in tutus twirl round and round,
While the grass giggles at the antics found.

Nature's a stage, and the jokes combine,
With each breeze whispering a punchline divine.
So come join the fun, don't miss the show,
Where serenity meets a delightful flow.

Dreaming Beyond the Canopy

Up in the trees, the monkeys play chess,
With bananas for pawns, who would've guessed?
Parrots squawk secrets with colorful flair,
While sloths in a hammock just don't have a care.

Clouds wear pajamas, drifting in style,
While sunlight tickles with a warming smile.
The vines have a party, swinging in glee,
And the owls wear glasses, sipping sweet tea.

Below in the meadow, the rabbits compete,
In a hopping contest, who's fastest on feet?
With daisies as judges, they cheer and they jeer,
Creating a joyful and raucous atmosphere.

This whimsical world spins and twirls,
With laughter and light, as each moment unfurls.
Beneath the green canopy, dreams take flight,
In a place where the silly feels just right.

Sunlit Journeys in Blooming Valleys

In valleys aflame with color and cheer,
Bumblebees waltz, swaying without fear.
Flowers gossip of secrets and dreams,
As butterflies giggle at grand schemes.

Hikers find broccoli shaped like a tree,
And ants in sunglasses sip their green tea.
The sun tickles noses and brightens the skies,
As everyone shares in laughter that flies.

With rivers that sparkle like diamonds at play,
Fish wear party hats to join in the fray.
The daisies nod knowingly, what a sight,
With whispers of joy in the warm, golden light.

Through valleys of laughter, each step we take,
Brings echoes of smiles like waves on a lake.
A journey so silly, so full of delight,
In this world where giggles make everything bright.

The Aesthetic of Untamed Beauty

Among wildflowers, the snails take a stroll,
With hats made of petals, oh what a goal!
They glide with such grace on the vibrant green,
While ladybugs cheer, it's a funny scene.

The wind whispers jokes to the trees that sway,
As squirrels debate on the best nut buffet.
Caterpillars fashion their costumes with flair,
To strut down the branch in a fashion so rare.

Grasshoppers host tap dance shows in the field,
While poppies are judges, their verdicts are sealed.
The sun chuckles brightly, a golden hostess,
As clouds watch the chaos, impressed with the jest.

Nature's an artist, and humor's the muse,
In this untamed place, there's nothing to lose.
With smiles stitched in each wild bloom and bend,
It's a vibrant tapestry where laughter won't end.

The Lasting Glow of Starry Nights

Beneath the stars we set the scene,
With marshmallows and a soda machine.
The moonlight beams, we toast our bread,
While raccoons giggle, dreaming in bed.

With glitter stains from cosmic snacks,
We blame the aliens for midnight cracks.
A comet flashes, we make a wish,
But all we get is a soggy fish!

The night is bright with laughter loud,
As fireflies dance beneath the cloud.
Each twinkling light, a joke on cue,
"Did you hear the one about the cow moo?"

So gather 'round, the night is fun,
Who needs the sun when stars outrun?
With giggles echoing in the air,
We claim this night is beyond compare!

Tranquility Sakred Beneath Infinite Skies

With lemonade and a picnic spread,
We laze around, not a single dread.
The clouds above, they seem to wink,
As squirrels conspire, and seagulls drink.

A gentle breeze carries tales of old,
Of all the legends that play out bold.
"Did you know," says a chipmunk with pride,
"That I once swam with a fish named Clyde?"

We sigh in joy, life's simple tricks,
While ants march by in their little flicks.
"Watch out for crumbs!" a wise man yells,
But ants can't resist those cookie smells.

Beneath the vastness, worries take flight,
In this bizarre, whimsical delight.
With laughter ringing from tree to tree,
We find our bliss, wild and carefree!

The Dance of the Fireflies

When dusk arrives, the fun begins,
As fireflies twinkle, and laughter spins.
They're not just bugs; they're disco stars,
Glowing in patterns like little cars.

We join the fun, chasing them round,
In a light-up game that knows no bound.
A firefly lands on my silly hat,
I declare it now a glowing cat!

While all the frogs croak in delight,
Encouraging us to dance all night.
"Join our croak-a-thon!" warns a sly toad,
"We might just start a slimy road!"

So under the stars, we jump and sway,
In a dance-off with fireflies, hip-hip-hooray!
With giggles erupting from every side,
This joyful chaos is our ride!

Reflections in the Quiet Waters

By the stream where the tadpoles leap,
I ponder life, then fall asleep.
The water splashes, wakes me with glee,
"Not again!" I cry, "Can't you see?"

With ripples dancing, secrets untold,
The fish swim past, being really bold.
"A race?" I ask, but they just laugh,
"Your slow-motion splashes are our warm bath!"

A frog jumps in, doing the backstroke,
While dragonflies buzz, plotting a joke.
"Why did you dive?" I ask with a stare,
"Because I wanted to swim with flair!"

In this quiet spot, where chuckles drift,
Nature's humor is the best gift.
So join the splash, embrace the play,
In the mirror of water, fun's here to stay!

Enchanted Realms of Delight

In lands where socks do dance with glee,
And rubber ducks hold court by the sea,
The sun wears shades and sips sweet tea,
While trees tell jokes as grand as can be.

This quirky place, where laughter's king,
And every cat can play the piano with zing,
The clouds form shapes of a trampoline,
With unicorns sharing ice cream in spring.

Where flowers wear hats, bright and wacky,
And grasshoppers play tunes that are snappy,
The stars at night waltz with a twinkle,
As moonbeams giggle, not a wink and a crinkle.

In this realm where whimsy is the law,
Balloons can talk, and the pizza has a flaw,
Here every moment is a silly surprise,
A place where joy stretches wide and flies.

The Tapestry of Endless Days

In the loom of time, where giggles weave,
And kittens hide in pockets to deceive,
A monkey swings by wearing a tie,
As jellybeans rain from a candy sky.

The clock strikes fun, not ticks nor tocks,
Where penguins play checkers in silly frocks,
Each hour bursts with cookies and cream,
While wishes float by like a daydream.

In this vibrant patchwork of cheer,
The whispers of squirrels make jokes that endear,
Marshmallow clouds against a blue backdrop,
It's a laughter festival that never will stop.

Every sunset a comic parade,
Where shadows dance and sunlight's made,
In this tapestry stitched with delight,
Every day's a carnival, oh what a sight!

Sunlit Corners of Tranquil Minds

In sunny nooks where serenades hum,
The bumblebees waltz, oh isn't that fun?
Where mushrooms wear scarves and daisies converse,
And garden gnomes prank with a wink and a verse.

Here tigers sip tea in the afternoon glow,
While frogs in tuxedos put on quite a show,
The breeze tells tales of mischief and mirth,
In this goofy haven, unbound by the earth.

Dandelions giggle when the wind blows just right,
And flip-flops tap dance into the night,
Such odd little corners that soothe and excite,
Wrapping the day in layers of light.

With laughter as fresh as the dew on the grass,
Every moment a circus, no hour will pass,
In these sunlit corners, we're all free to unwind,
Two beads of sunshine, oh what's left behind!

The Breath of Morning Glories

As dawn unfolds with a wink and a grin,
The daisies chuckle, let the antics begin,
With toast that can dance and coffee that sings,
Morning glories, oh joy that this day brings.

Chirpy birds wearing hats, how quaint!
Chasing buttercups, what a frivolous point,
Each baby's breath tickles with glee,
In the giggle of dawn, it's just you and me.

Bumblebees bustle with plans so absurd,
In the bubble of laughter, it's never unheard,
As the sun's golden rays play peek-a-boo,
Morning glories bloom in the brightest hue.

With every petal telling tales oh-so-fine,
A garden of chuckles, a real favorite line,
The breath of each morning, so fresh and so funny,
In this whimsical world, oh how sweet and sunny!

Beneath the Canopy of Stars

Under the twinkling, winking sky,
Squirrels debating, oh my oh my!
Grasshoppers dance, losing their beat,
While fireflies zip, making it sweet.

Laughter echoes, a joyous sound,
As cats plot mischief, prowling around.
With stars as our audience, we jest,
In this nighttime show, we are the best!

A raccoon juggling with flair and style,
While owls hoot a catchy new dial.
Join the fun, let worries disperse,
Life's a playful, whimsical verse.

So here we lay, beneath the blooms,
With nature's weirdness dispelling glooms.
If laughter's the key, then take your shot,
In a realm where giggles can't be bought!

A Tapestry of Joy

Threads of laughter weave through the air,
Kittens cornering shadows with flair.
Clouds wear smiles, fluffy and bright,
Tickling the sun, such a delight!

In a patch where daisies dance,
A duckling's waddle turns into a prance.
Bees in a conga line buzzing away,
Seems they're ready to party all day!

Banana peels wait for slips with glee,
While turtles argue who's faster, oh me!
Joy spills like soda, fizzing about,
In this zany world, there's no doubt!

So let's gather round for a giggly feast,
With pies and jokes, oh it's never ceased!
Each moment a stitch in this yarn so fine,
In this tapestry, your laughter will shine.

The Serene Sanctuary

In a nook where the chubby squirrels munch,
An occasional duck takes things in a crunch.
Sunrays tickle the lazy old trees,
While turtles ponder world mysteries.

A rock band of frogs croaks out their tunes,
As daisies sway to the rhythm of moons.
Clouds look on in bewildered surprise,
With giggles erupting from beetle spies!

Dandelion wishes ride soft gentle breeze,
Whispering secrets to the buzzing bees.
Nature's own comedy plays out on stage,
As rabbits perform, flipping the page.

When laughter's the theme, worries recede,
In this haven, there's laughter indeed.
So come on and laugh, let out a cheer,
In this space, my friend, nothing to fear!

Fields of Gentle Hope

In fields where wildflowers wear silly hats,
Bunnies rehearse for their acrobats.
The sun beams down, with a wink and a grin,
While ladybugs gossip; oh, where to begin?

Butterflies giggle, their colors ablaze,
As they flutter through sunlit maze.
A snail races blind, with dreams in its shell,
Holding on tightly to triumphs to tell.

Here, joy is the currency, spent without care,
Tickles of laughter float up in the air.
Fields of wonder where silliness reigns,
Nature's own playground, where no one complains.

So prance through the meadows, take off your shoes,
Embrace the wackiness, sing silly blues!
In these gentle fields, let your heart open wide,
For hope blooms best when laughter's your guide!

The Harmony of Birds in Flight

With feathers bright, they make a show,
Singing tunes only they know.
They sport their hats of many hues,
Making humans sing the blues.

A dance midair, oh what a sight,
They squawk and dive, a feathery fight.
Yet when they land, they lose their charm,
Looking more like a feathered farm.

Chirping jokes, they share a laugh,
In the trees, they craft their craft.
Who knew that wings could be so wise?
As they plot to steal our fries!

These winged clowns in bright display,
Nobody sees the humor's sway.
In their whispers soft and sweet,
Laughing while they grab a treat.

Infinite Blossoms at Dusk

Petals dance, oh what a scene,
Like cotton candy, bright and clean.
Bumbling bees with heavy loads,
Trip over blooms, create new roads.

Sunset paints each flower's face,
One looks grumpy, what a case!
Roses giggle, violets smirk,
As night descends, they still work.

A daisy trips on its own stem,
While lilies plot a little gem.
They make bouquets for passing bees,
And end up dusted by the breeze.

In this garden, laughter grows,
While petals flutter, nature knows.
Each blossom has its secret game,
But in their jokes, they bring no shame.

Chasing Sunbeams and Moonlit Streams

Sunbeams race with shadows in tow,
Splashing light like a sweet-flow show.
Frog on a log, what an odd sight,
Catch me if you can—oh, what a fright!

Moonlit streams, they giggle and gleam,
For fish will dance in a silver dream.
Each ripple a shout, responsive at best,
As they trade spots like a lively jest.

Catching sunrays as they play,
Fish roles confuse, oh what a day!
The sun's not shy, it takes a dive,
While minnows strive to stay alive!

The twilight winks, the stars join in,
Wishing upon fish with a silly grin.
In this silly chase, what fun it seems,
Dancing beings all wrapped in dreams.

Portraits of a Seraphic Landscape

Hills painted green with laughter loud,
Clouds taking naps, feeling quite proud.
Sunflowers pose, like models divine,
Waving at clouds for that perfect line.

Mountains chuckle, their peaks are tall,
Telling tales of the great and small.
The grass tickles toes, in playful delight,
While crickets serenade throughout the night.

Rainbows paint smiles across the sky,
As colors argue who's the flyest guy.
Each color's claim, a riotous fight,
Ending up in giggles, oh what a sight!

In this frame of mischief and cheer,
The landscape twirls, spreading joy near.
A masterpiece where silliness reigns,
In every stroke, laughter remains.

www.ingramcontent.com/pod-product-compliance
Lightning Source LLC
Chambersburg PA
CBHW072120070526
44585CB00016B/1509